The Houses That Raise Our Girls

#FemaleNOTFeemale

The Houses That Raise Our Girls

#FemaleNOTFeemale

Sherri Jefferson

To every female. . . past, present, and future.

#FemaleNotFEEmale

From her house to the church house.
From the schoolhouse to the courthouse.
In the jailhouse to be warehoused.
Each of these houses ("systems") are responsible for
the successes _or_ failures of our girls.

 #FemaleNotFEEmale

ABOUT
I AM #FemaleNotFEEmale

#FemaleNotFEEmale believes that all women and children were born #FREEmale. #FemaleNotFEEmale is an initiative utilizing four strategic/action-oriented campaigns to promote justice and opportunity for victims of child sex slavery and human trafficking in the United States. We are advocating to dismantle the Prostitution to Prison Pipeline.

1. We are advocating against prosecuting children as prostitutes and for providing treatment and services in mental health, substance abuse, and healthcare.

2. We are advocating against jailhouse incarceration and for unrestrictive safe houses that offer educational, health, and preventive services.

3. We are advocating for a Fair Criminal Records Reporting Act, which like credit histories, will delete criminal records as a result of prostitution or related offenses. Expungement and Restriction do not delete records, it merely seals them.

4. We are advocating to prevent collateral consequences associated with a criminal record which impacts the H.E.M.S: Housing, Health, Education, Employment, Maintenance and Support services of victims of child sexual exploitation and domestic minor sex trafficking.

www.FemaleNOTFeemale.com

PREFACE

I believe that every female was born into this world as a _**free**_male not a _**fee**_male. Her life is precious, her opinion matters, and she is valued. In a world that is full of uncertainty and untenable obstacles, we must invest time and resources into the lives of all girls. Today, our girls are our sisters and daughters, but tomorrow some may choose to become mothers and/or professionals in the workplace and they need guidance, wisdom and protection. In my years as an advocate for social change, I have witnessed firsthand and have personal knowledge about the plights faced by girls. The challenges can sometimes be daunting.

If we view the lives and outcomes of girls between the ages of 4–18 through almost any critical lens, we clearly see that our parenting, pastoral care, educational services, rehabilitative and health care systems are broken. The disproportionate representation and gender inequity goes beyond breaking the glass ceiling.

An easy read, The Houses that Raise Our Girls is a smart and practical examination of the 6Ps (**Parents, Pastors, Principals, Police, Prosecutors and Prison**) that house girls in America. I deftly combine wisdom from my professional experiences working with girls who are victims of the prison pipelines of school, poverty, mental illness, sexual exploitation and abuse and prostitution.

The book combines thought-provoking insight about the role of the 6Ps in the rearing of girls, and candid descriptions of pop cultural trends and societal norms that define our girls. A straightforward conversation, the reader will finish this short read on fire and ready, willing, and capable of taking back what is being stolen from us – the innocence of our girls!

Beyond the Book is a supplement that includes a study guide and resources.

I wrote this book in Spanish and English to reach a wider audience so that I may help to change the lives of all girls. I hope to bridge the gaps and the language barriers that divide us.

"For these are all our children.
We will all profit by, or pay for, whatever they become."
-James Baldwin

 #FemaleNotFEEmale

INTRODUCTION

#FemaleNOTFeemale understands the hurt and pain of the communities and their sympathizers who are victims of the pipelines that deliver our girls from the schoolhouse to the jailhouse. The pipelines of poverty, juvenile prostitution (aka sexual abuse and domestic child sexual exploitation), and mental health plague girls of color and the poor. Over the last decade, these pipelines have created an increase in the number of girls displaced from their homes, schools and communities. Many of these girls are now in juvenile detention facilities/prisons, have dropped out of school as a result of being pushed out or are single-parents on public welfare. Equally, some have been able to overcome the barriers of the pipelines and are enrolled in college or vocational schools and are gainfully employed.

With that being said, #FemaleNOTFeemale promotes accountability and responsibility regarding the issues that plague our girls and their communities. We cannot live in excuses, denial and justification. We know that racism, sexism, and classism is real. #FemaleNOTFeemale believes in the premise of making life choices and judgments that become the real determining factors of the destiny of our children. We want to teach girls that sometimes it is more important to focus on how you treat yourself and not how others treat you. Sometimes, unknowingly, we give people permission and a license to mistreat us. It is important that we teach our girls not to open the door to some forms of abuse.

For example, we must teach our girls how to value their bodies and to be in control of their own minds; we must teach our girls about healthy relationships and the importance of self-esteem. Furthermore, if our girls attain their academic standing, do not engage in criminality, and are productive citizens, it makes it difficult for anyone to engage in mistreatment. If and when it occurs, the remedies are and should be swift and penal. Therefore, if we make them victims of their circumstances they will be less likely to overcome life challenges.

Racism and classism are realities for our girls. However, we need to be equally concerned about how our girls end up in the child welfare and juvenile justice system at our hands. If we can curtail or prevent the number of children entering child protective services/DFCS and juvenile detention, then we would have accomplished a major task.

Prevention and intervention are not legislative issues they are moral issues. Teen pregnancy, dropping out of school, and delinquency are choices that are either made by our girls and them alone because of acts committed by strangers or the acts of their parents or guardians that includes social ills like abuse, neglect, and mistreatment, etc. We must teach our girls to press toward life's greatest opportunities and they can be equipped with the tools to be victors and not victims. Girls of this social media era can be transformed by the renewing of **our** minds and how **we** approach parenting, providing pastoral care and services and, educational and disciplinary methods. Girls of this social media era represent the generation of Living the Dream. The choice of education or incarceration is up to the 6Ps (Parents, Pastors, Principals, Police, Prosecutors and Prisons – alternatively Physicians, Psychologist and Pharmaceutical companies).

An easy-to-read, #FemaleNOTFeemale recognizes the importance of protecting the identities of girls with hopes that they will have productive lives free from continued reminders of their past. Toward that end, our material excludes names and personal information. The emphasis of *The Houses that Raise Our Girls* is to highlight some of the obstacles that plague our girls and to offer some suggestions that might help to improve their circumstances by holding the 6Ps (Parents, Pastors, Principals, Police, Prosecutors and Prisons – alternatively Physicians, Psychologist and Pharmaceutical companies) accountable and responsible for their role in the lives of girls. We also deliver tools that girls need for survival. This material focuses on the crux of the community concerns, which seeks justice and human rights, but also #FemaleNOTFeemale uses this platform as a call to action and change.

#FemaleNOTFeemale

Project 3Ps

Parents, Pastors, and Principals

Results 3Rs

Rears, Reinforces, and Reimburses

#FemaleNOTFeemale

Parents, Pastors and Principals

Shaping the Future of Girls

#FemaleNOTFeemale: The Parent (Rear)

Who is responsible for the rearing of our girls? Rearing begins at home. Therefore, parents or guardians are responsible for the rearing of our girls. Almost everything we expect our girls to learn about love, the meaning of family, self-identification and the importance of education and learning starts at home. So what happens when the home life is compromised by drugs, alcohol, abuse or neglect? Who steps in to help raise our girls? Where are kinfolk? Where are the grandmothers, aunts and cousins? Where are other female role models from within the fabric of the home life? When that is absent where is the church or school community? We are responsible for the Houses that Raise Our Girls!

Unique to the American experience is the role that social media and entertainment, divorce, single parenting, early child care providers and nanny services are playing in the rearing of girls. It has become more difficult to raise powerful girls in a society where they lack positive female and male role models.

Our girls did not ask to be born. Our girls did not ask for the collateral consequences associated with the burdens of being born into *this* society. Our girls did not ask for parents who abandon them or a society who fails them. Parents you are responsible for building the *House* that raises your girls. The Houses that Raise Our Girls must have a *design* or a *plan*. What is your plan for your daughter, niece or the female in your life? What do you desire of her life and what course of action are you taking to ensure that she will be a proud, loving, and productive female in our society?

The House that Raises Our Girls must have a site and a foundation. Parents where is your site and what is in your foundation? Is your site located in an inner city or urban community? Is your site located in the housing developments or projects of a major city? Is your site located in a rural trailer park community? Is your site located in an affluent suburban community? Surely, you do not desire to raise your daughter on a toxic waste site? What type of foundation are you using to effectively build the house that raises your girls? Is your foundation premised upon being family-oriented and being truthful, while possessing integrity and building self-esteem? Is your foundation premised upon love and not hate, accountability and responsibility as well as open, candid, and honest communications with your girls? The Houses that Raise Our Girls must be built upon a solid foundation.

Once you have designed or created a plan, located your site, and laid your foundation, you must be subject to inspection. Your inspectors (society) may approve or disapprove of your plan, you may have defects in your design and in your foundation. Be willing to make the necessary changes early in your development. Lest, you see the fruits of your labor later in life when your daughter is ill equipped to survive or thrive in this world.

The Houses that Raise Our Girls must be fully equipped to deal with the issues of society. Like with any structure, the Houses that Raise Our Girls must be equipped with plumbing, heating and cooling systems, and flooring. How does this translate to raising girls? Well, let us examine. To be effective in this society, we must instill morals, values, and respect in our girls. Our girls must be 'wired' emotionally, psychologically, and mentally. We must equip them with the tools that enable them to take a stand and defend. Our girls must be equipped with the ability to read, to write, to comprehend, to calculate, and to use logic among many other necessities. We must teach our girls how to fend for themselves, and how to cook, clean, sew, and devise and maintain a financial budget. The Houses that Raise Our Girls must teach our girls how to develop a plan of action for their own lives and set goals and agendas and be capable of fulfilling their goals.

The Houses that Raise Our Girls must install insulation because every girl needs protection. The protection required must come from positive male and female role models. Insulation provides a comfortable environment for girls that is consistent with protective barriers from the coldness of this world. The Houses that Raise Our Girls is responsible for preventing our girls from experiencing harm when we allow people to enter their lives that sexually assault and rape them, beat and mistreat them, break their inner-spirits by disrespecting them, and engaging in name calling like referring to girls as bitches and whores, or suggesting that they will never be anything in life. The power of our tongue determines the future of our young. The Houses that Raise Our Girls must insulate them from societal ills and while we cannot guarantee 100% protection, using quality material can ensure the best results.

Once we have completed the insulation, the Houses that Raise Our Girls must complete the drywall and interior fixtures. Seaming the walls together is necessary for a finished look and for preparing the walls for paint. Our girls must be complete. The Houses that Raise Our Girls must make sure that before our girls enter society that they are seamed together, that there are no cracks in their walls (mental, emotional, psychological and spiritual development). We must make sure that they have not been broken by what we have failed to do for their growth and development. The open seam will be seen on the outside. Outsiders will be able to look in and use the cracks to their advantage. This is why so many girls look for love in so many of the wrong places and why they become victims of unhealthy relationships. Conversely, this is also why some girls become pregnant and are met with the choice of abortion because parents did not teach about choices of abstinence and contraception. Among girls of color, especially African-American girls, abortions have become a form of birth control. The Houses that Raise Our Girls must emphasize planning for parenthood and educate girls about choices that prevent ending the lives of children. Abortions are a traumatizing experience and mental health services are not provided for aftercare. After having abortions, some of these girls engage in self-destructive behaviors.

Once we have completed the exterior and interior, we are ready to install flooring and countertops. The Houses that Raise Our Girls must have a solid flooring system so that girls may withstand the uncertainty of this world and they must be able to stand strong against adversity. This is not the time to cut corners and reduce the quality of material used. There are multiple flooring materials to choose from, some hardwood and some planked or maybe carpeting. There is builder grade, residential and commercial quality. The Houses that Raise Our Girls must set aside a budget to purchase only the best that money can buy. We must prioritize our income and earnings so that we spend our money and use our resources wisely toward building character, integrity, and instilling morals, value and respect. If a parent is more interested in having their hair styled, wearing fancy clothing, and exploring the dating scene while their daughter hair is unkempt and her clothing are uncleaned and she lacks hygiene than that girl will learn to set the same priorities or lack thereof as she ages.

Just like structuring the interior of a house, what we put on the inside of our girls is everlasting. We are responsible for making sure that as parents that they feel confident, strong, and secure within themselves. To be strong and confident is not weakening to their male counterparts. To be strong and confident is not to discredit or disarm their male counterparts. Rather, it is a means to aid our girls to survive and thrive in a dominate world using their education, experience and employable skills. Our girls must learn early in life that education is a human rights issue not a social, political or economic issue. The power and ability to secure a quality education starts with the foundation that we lay at home.

The Houses that Raise Our Girls must prepare girls to compete globally not just locally. This means reading from the womb, engaging our girls in S.T.E.M. programs that prepare our girls in science, technology, engineering and mathematics. It means teaching our girls not to be afraid of scientific formulas and mathematical equations. Our girls are not born incompetent in the field of S.T.E.M. They lack competency because we are either afraid to prepare them, unwilling to prepare them or lack the knowledge and resources to secure an educational program that offers S.T.E.M. Alternatively, we are too lazy to take them to programs that are within our reach.

The Houses that Raise Our Girls must install fixtures throughout the house. When building a home, we put fixtures in the bathroom and the bedrooms such as ceiling fans and lighting. Meaning, we must add value to our girls by letting their light shine to the world. We must only use quality material that will outlast even the worst storm. Adding value does not mean spending every penny you saved. You can add value to your daughter by shopping at consignment shops, estate sales or other second hand venues and purchase items that are worth more but cost less. Adding value means communicating to your daughter or the female in your life that she is a winner; it means communicating her abilities and stressing her greatness. It means advocating for her and her beliefs. It means helping her set and then achieve her goals.

The Houses that Raise Our Girls can do this in the smallest amount of time, a drive to school, a walk in the park or to the store, while styling her hair during the evening or morning hours, and by watching a television program with her that promotes her self-worth and awareness. It means setting aside a moment of the day to put down the phone, log off the computer or tell someone that your daughter has a need that must be addressed. It means adding value in words and deeds. Adding value means helping her to learn to accept herself and love herself. It means teaching her not to compare herself to others. The earlier we instill these principles into our girls the better off they will be in learning to love and accept their strengths and weakness.

When our girls seek an interest in boys, we must be open, honest and candid about relationships and sexual encounters. During these times, we must also discuss date rape and the challenges of physical, emotional, mental, and psychological attachments with boys. We must discuss abstinence and safe sex with our girls. While we may want them to say "no", they may say "yes." They must be prepared to face and deal with the consequences of HIV/AIDS, STDs and an unwanted pregnancy. It is a disservice to tell a girl that she is too young to bear a child, but not too young to have sex. Too often, we ignore issues of birth control and abortions become the norm. Then, our girls are denied mental health counseling regarding the death of their unborn.

When girls fall short of expectations, be mindful about how you discipline. There is a difference between discipline and punishment. Words can destroy a child more than physical abuse. If she is subject to arrest and/or incarceration, do not avoid visitation, she requires that attention. During her incarceration, provide her with letters of encouragement, and remind her that she is loved. Talk to her about her experiences – ask questions! Many of our girls are victims of sexual assault by court officials, probation officers, and male and female officers as well as inmates.

We must teach our girls about self- awareness to transform their self-esteem into self-love. We must teach our girls how self-hate transforms into self-destruction. We must communicate with our girls to garner an understanding of what it means to be raised in a social media era that subjects children to instantaneous shame and humiliation, and cyberbullying and in-school bullying. Girls must learn how to develop healthy friendships and relationships with others. Our girls must learn how to stand against immorality, inhumane acts, and abusive conduct or behavior.

There exists a thin line between gossip and defamation of character. Our girls must learn the difference when spreading rumors about others that are baseless and lacking in truth. Equally, when our girls communicate truth, it should be done to edify and not harm. Every girl needs someone to defend her honor. As parents, be willing to defend your child, never subjecting her to embarrassment, humiliation or shame. Be willing to attend parent-teacher conferences and court appearances, and be willing to meet with her adversaries who oppose her. Create dialogue and extend an olive branch to her foes to build relationships. Teach her to understand the power of forgiveness.

Every house requires mirrors and after completing installation of fixtures, mirrors and showers doors are added to the home. The Houses that Raise Our Girls must teach our girls to love what they see in the mirror. Let us be honest, the world sees what they perceive as ugly and beauty. The Houses that Raise Our Girls must be candid, open, and honest. If your child looks different, promote her best! Do not focus on her differences, but do not hide their existence and leave her to the world to be defined. Looks and hygiene are critical and must be taught at home.

After completing the interior of the home and adding furnishing most people are ready to finalize their landscaping. The outer appearance is very important in this social media era that our girls live and thrive. However, we must teach them how to survive with their outer beauty and how some people may take advantage of their outer beauty. Girls must learn that their value cannot be measured in dollars and cents but in their overall appearance.

We must instill in our girls that the value of their clothing is not as important as the person wearing them. A $200.00 tight and form fitting dress has no added value to the wearer. The cost of the dress gives no guarantee that the wearer will be respected by her peers or others; it will not guarantee employment opportunities in the future. The cost of the dress will not prove that the wearer is smarter or more talented than the person wearing a pair of $6 jeans from a consignment or second hand store. Surely, appearance in some circles goes a long way. However, if we teach values and priority than our girls will feel like a million dollars no matter what they wear. We have so many girls who knowingly engage in acts of sexual activity in exchange for a new pair of shoes, handbag, sunglasses, or a pair of sneakers because we failed to teach them to value their bodies over material possessions.

Parents and guardians are the first 'systems' or owners of the Houses that Raise Our Girls. When they operate in accordance to some of these suggestions and prepare our girls for the world, then the other systems (pastors and schools) will have an easier task of raising our girls when they enter their houses.

#FemaleNOTFeemale: The Church (Reinforce)

The Houses that Raise Our Girls includes the church house. The church is capable of reinforcing and instilling values, morals and teaching respect to girls. The church can prepare girls to respect authority and build character. While some people have no religious or spiritual belief system, respectfully most girls in America leave their house to go to the church house. There was a time when the church provided programs and services to aid families in need. The church house was part of the community and addressed political, social, and economic issues for the betterment of the community. Today, in many urban and rural corridors the church is self-serving and has chosen to ignore the plight of the community. Many of the pastors, preachers, priest or reverends do not reside in the community where their churches are located. Hence, the community is not the congregation and there is no commitment to provide programs or services to uplift the people.

When this system fails, our girls and the community suffers. Over the last two decades we see the breakdown of the urban and rural churches. Sure there exist plenty of mega-churches, but there exist mega problems in the urban and rural communities. Girls within these communities suffer from abuse, neglect, mistreatment and maltreatment. Where do they go? If mother is on drugs and their father is incarcerated where will they go? How will girls handle the challenges of the D.I.G[1] mentality? Who and where will they turn?

The church house was an institution of the community that served its members. So many girls have no resources or programs available. The churches are only open in some communities on Sunday for service, maybe

---

[1] drugs, drunkenness, ignorance, illiteracy, guns and greed

Wednesday for Bible study and maybe on a Friday. The weekday services are generally no more than 2 hours during the evening. So what programs and services are available for girls? Who meets their spiritual needs? Who helps them to overcome their spiritual demons because even girls possess demonic intrusion or anxieties that causes some of them to suffer from eating disorders, depression, suicide, hypertension, and hyper-sexuality.

There existed a time when people could go to the church to get guidance. Today, many churches operate like a 9-5 business. It is the fault of their congregation that their system fails the girls. However, for purposes of this material, it is important that the church is called out to go beyond its charismatic, self-serving, conferencing and book promoting programs, to address the needs and concerns of girls. The church house is a system that is involved in raising of our girls. If our girls are suffering it is because the church system has failed them too. Surely not all churches, many churches exist in the urban, rural, and some suburban corridors of America that have failed and have fallen short of meeting the needs of girls.

Attend any church in an urban and rural community and look around. You will see that women represent the majority of the congregation. Women represent the little girls who suffer in silence until their adulthood. If we find means to provide the programs and services that girls need in their youth, we will not have altars across the country with women weeping from unresolved hurts and pains from their childhood.

The Houses that Raise Our Girls includes the church house and we must demand that the church fulfill its Godly principles of providing our girls with programs and services that includes becoming part of the faith based community outreach to help girls deal with anxiety, anger management, rape, abuse, mental health illness, drugs and alcohol, and suicide and depression. Some churches are gifted with the ability to provide counseling services. Therefore, our girls should not suffer in juvenile detention and prison facilities to attain the services that the faith-based community can provide. Deprived and delinquent girls can be court ordered to enter church and faith-based programs. Please get involved and help our girls.

#FemaleNOTFeemale: The School (Reimburse)

School should be preparatory grounds for preparing girls to become productive citizens so that girls can be contributors to and reimburse society. There are three pipelines that adversely affect girls in America. The school-to-prison pipeline is one of the pipelines due to disparate school discipline. According to the U.S. Department of Education black girls are six times more likely to be suspended than white girls.

Many urban and rural communities, especially the minority community pled for teachers and school administrators of color with hopes that the similarities would mean that their children will attain a better education or experience a greater learning outcome. However, from Atlanta, Georgia where their school system engaged in a decade long cheating scandal to the city of Detroit school district scandal, disproves that teachers and administrators of color provide children of color with a better education, today. Since these districts and others resolved to cheating for academic advancement, it may suggest that these school districts lack faith in children of color and their ability to excel academically.

The schoolhouse is one of the Houses that Raise Our Girls. We look to them to share the role of nurturing our girls. After all, girls spend more time in school than they do in their own houses. Most school district began their weekday at 7 a.m. and end at 4 p.m. and it is a problem when schools elect to use police, court systems, and the prisons to discipline children entrusted to their care, control, and custody.

Some teachers have personal problems of their own and some come to school with preconceived thoughts about girls, especially girls of color. However, in conversing with girls, many have alleged that teachers of color are no more understanding of their plight than their white counterparts. Why? Could it be that many of them have little empathy for girls due to their own upbringing that is based upon a lack of mother-daughter relationship or lack of father-daughter relationship? Is it based on economics or social class? Examine a so-called mecca like Atlanta and its surrounding school districts. Look at the number of students' subject to their school to prison pipeline and examine the districts where they are subject to detention. Most of these children are detained in Clayton, Fulton and DeKalb school districts, which represents the majority of the African-American student bodies. The practices are similar in New York City, Detroit, and Newark.

The schoolhouse is one of the Houses that Raises Our Girls. African-American children represent less than 25% of the general school-aged population in the United States. However, in most jurisdictions in this country, they represent more than 60% of the children subject to arrest, conviction, and incarceration for school-related offenses[2]. Overall, these students are subject to in and out of

---

[2] Lewin, Tamar. "Black Students Face More Discipline, Data Suggests" http://www.nytimes.com/2012/03/06/education/black-students-face-more-harsh-discipline-data-shows.html?_r=0 March 6, 2012; Criminal Justice Fact Sheet. http://www.naacp.org/pages/criminal-justice-fact-sheet (2015); United States Department of Education Office of Civil Rights. School Discipline. http://ocrdata.ed.gov/Downloads/CRDC-School-Discipline-Snapshot.pdf March 2014

school suspension, expulsion and/or referrals to law enforcement within the same school as their white peers.

The dismantling of the school–to-prison pipeline is not only necessary but if not dismantled, then it poses a threat to national security. We are criminalizing the behaviors of our future leaders in the field of law, science, math, engineering, and technology. This segment of society is purposefully, intentionally, wantonly, and maliciously being excluded from global competition. By criminalizing and incarcerating girls, we disqualify them from successful completion of traditional educational programs and from attending college. Therefore, we are preventing them from entering professional careers.

Further, the United States military services relies heavily on recruitment of high school students from urban and rural communities. Many of these students are victims of the school-to-prison pipeline where children go from their house, to the schoolhouse, to the jailhouse and courthouse, just to be warehoused. By indiscriminately criminalizing the behaviors of girls and subjecting these children to arrest for school-related offenses, some girls face ineligibility for armed services.

The schoolhouse can use counseling services and create in-school programs to better understand behavioral problems. In-school suspension should be more than sitting in a classroom and doing class assignments. It should include a disciplinary approach program that seeks to garner information and offer programs to target conduct and behavioral problems. Schools have more police officers on campus than school counselors. Once upon a time, school counselors were the first steps to addressing in-school disciplinary problems. Through use of school counselors, parents, teachers and social workers learned about sexual abuse, pregnancies, maltreatment, and other issues experienced by children. School counselors offered programs and services. Today, most schools lack counselors and some counselors are serving in administrative capacities that are the equivalent of the school secretary.

Once upon a time, schools offered health education courses that addressed sex education. These courses were offered in middle schools to educate girls and boys about abstinence, birth control, and self-awareness. Most school districts no longer offer these courses. Girls who become pregnant feel ashamed, embarrassed and experience humiliation. They act out in class and then are pushed out of school without anyone addressing their experiences or their pregnancy. Many have become pregnant through rape, incest, and sex trafficking.

Disparities exist in girls of color. Commission report after report demonstrates that Latinas, Mexicans, and African-Americans girls are more likely than white students to be suspended, arrested, and expelled from school. Despite the private and public research and federal data, there is no change in the outcome for African-Americans. The cries to dismantle the school-to-prison pipeline are not new. Since the Columbine High School shooting in 1999 and the implementation of zero-tolerance guidelines, schools across America have become prisons where children are inmates, the principal serves as the warden and teachers are the jailers. The use of militarized police to secure the schools is akin to the practice of placing shooters on the roof of prisons while inmates have recreation time in the yard.

Contrary to the misrepresentations associated with urban schools, the schools dominated by girls of color are less likely than their white peers to have Columbine and Sandy Hook experiences. Why are Latinas, African-American and Mexican girls more likely to be suspended, expelled or arrested? Every day in America girls are faced with the fear of losing their core liberties under the U.S. Constitution for engaging in school-related acts like talking back to a teacher, having a cat fight on the playground, or even singing a song or writing a poem that is deemed inappropriate. Girls are arrested for engaging in acts of giving a classmate an aspirin for mensural cramps, smoking cigarettes in the restroom or fighting on the school bus.

These measures of discipline are punitive. School districts can use parent-teacher conferences and in-school disciplinary actions to address these acts, which do not invoke the use of expulsion or referral to law enforcement. However, the handcuffing and arrest of a six-year old little girl for having a tantrum are not only measures that are extreme and outrageous, but equally abridge and infringe upon the Constitutional safeguards afforded to students. Since 1969 in *Tinker v Des Moines School District*, the United States Supreme Court has held that "Students do not lose their constitutional rights at the schoolhouse door."

To that end, some teachers in America's public schools are academically inexperienced, ill-trained, unprepared to handle behavioral issues, and incapable of handling the day-to-day stresses associated with teaching. It appears that the problems lie with preparatory college programs, which include proprietary schools and online programs as well as with school personnel and administrators who fail to weed-out these individuals during their program studies or after a probationary period. There exist tenure teachers who do not belong in the classroom. The nationally publicized Atlanta Public Schools' cheating scandal demonstrates some of the problems associated with teachers in urban school settings, which includes struggling with classroom management, inability to successfully perform lesson and unit planning and meeting the academic demands. These problems extend to addressing disciplinary matters.

Aside from evidence of blatant discrimination and disparity in addressing school discipline, America must weigh the mental, emotional and psychological impact associated with early police-citizen encounters and the arrest and incarceration of school-aged girls. Everyone is responsible for the demise of girls – parents, pastors (faith-based community), principals, police, prosecutors and prison personnel. Today, schools and law enforcement hold children accountable and responsible for the failures of their parents and communities. The nation cannot sit idle and pass around Commission reports and studies because that will not solve this problem. What will America gain by failing its most vulnerable segment of society? What will become of America if we continue to neglect our girls?

#FemaleNOTFeemale

Project 3Ps

Police, Prosecutor and Prison

Results 3Rs

Respond, Reprieve, and Rehabilitate

#FemaleNOTFeemale

Police, Prosecutor and Prison

The Pipeline Participants

#FemaleNOTFeemale: Police (Respond)

Police are first responders to balancing law and order. Police are not prosecutors, lawyers, judges or the jury. Most police officers are properly trained to engage in militarized tactics, address urban and rural warfare and embattled communities. Alternatively, most police officers are trained to deal with daily interactions with members of society with respect, professionalism, and customer service.

Once upon a time, police would engage in community outreach that enabled them to know the communities and residents that they served. Today, policing is more complex with officers traveling afar to manage the affairs of urban and rural communities with little or no interaction with local residents or knowledge of the community. This method of policing is problematic because it creates a 'them' versus 'us' mentality that is built upon lack of knowledge, mistrust, and stereotypes.

When police knew the residents and communities that they served fewer people were subject to negative police-citizen encounters. This is particularly true when dealing with youthful offenders. Once upon a time members of law enforcement would return a child to their parents or neighbors for instruction and constructive criticism and discipline. Today, few community police engage in these practices and those who continue are generally in small townships and affluent communities. To balance this point, the make-up of many urban and rural communities may make this task difficult because of lack of parenting, lack of pastoral services and lack of community and educational services.

Police are given enormous power and discretion. When used properly and fairly, police are able to determine whether youthful offenders should be subject to arrest or verbal warnings. Police are encouraged to steer on this side of policing when dealing with youthful offenders, especially girls. No. On the contrary, this is not a request for preferential treatment based on gender, rather it is a request to consider the prejudicial outcomes that stem from the arrest and unnecessary detention of children, especially girls. Why subject youthful offenders to arrest and damage their future with criminal charges and a criminal record that will generally result in dismissal if pursued against an adult. Our children, especially girls, are prone to engage in youthful offenses like cat fights involving no weapons, verbal exchanges, and the use of social media and telephones to display their hurt, bitterness or anger toward another.

Some girls may use social media to exploit their own nude photos unaware of the legal consequences. It is unfortunate that moral legislation and judicial activism stands in the way of commonsense approaches to dealing with youth, especially girls. We need police to remain focus and to be steadfast in aiding the communities that they serve and understanding youthful offenders. Most youthful offenders lack the criminal mind or intent to commit a delinquent act and few understand the consequences associated with their actions. Few understand that their first cat fight would cause an arrest or that smoking a cigarette in the restroom or making out with a boy would lead to a criminal charge of lewd behavior.

To subject these youthful offenders to criminal arrest for bogus charges that would never stand against an adult is criminal. Arresting children for battery, harassing communications for sending "too many text or email messages" or arrest on charges of terrorist threats for asserting "I will kick your butt" was never the legislative intent and is unconscionable. Respectfully, as members of law enforcement when you know better, you must do better! Your service to communities goes beyond arresting people. Police must protect, serve, and respect citizens and that goes beyond any slogan on a police vehicle.

To that end, there are many officers who understand their role, duty, and commitment to the communities that they serve. Policing is a difficult job and it is more difficult when officers are forced to make arrest, no matter how bogus the charges, to support a revenue generating system for their departments and locales.

Police are first responders and as such #FemaleNOTFeemale respectfully ask that you respond with empathy to the communities that you serve. We ask that you learn to understand that youthful offenders are children. Some children, including girls, may engage in violent acts, however that is not norm according to statistics available by the FBI and other reporting agencies. Our girls are not monsters. They are human beings with bright futures and many need guidance, wisdom, love, and protection. You can make a difference!

#FemaleNOTFeemale: Prosecutor (Reprieve)

The role of the prosecutor is to officially charge or prosecute a person for the commission of a crime and to balance the scales of justice. Prosecutors are vested with enormous authority that governs whether a person who has been arrested will be officially charged with a crime and face conviction. In their daily activities prosecutors are given an opportunity to utilize the services of in-house investigators and to examine police reports and witness statements before deciding whether to commence with prosecution (to seek to indict and present a case to a grand jury).

Every day in America, children are arrested for youthful offenses. Many of their arrest are submitted to the prosecutor for prosecution. Most of these offenses are nonviolent. Prosecutors also have the ability and responsibility to avoid prejudicial abuse of discretion and prosecution. Meaning, that they must make sure that they are not using race, gender, ethnicity or any prejudices to knowingly advance claims against people or to avoid prosecution based upon these variables. They have the authority to dismiss cases and go beyond restrictions and expungement to seek deletion of arrest records so that youthful offenders do not spend the rest of their lives answering to the call of "felon," "ex-con," "troublemaker," "problem kid," "convict," "criminal," "whore" or "prostitute."

Many children, especially girls return to their respective communities after being arrested depressed, embarrassed, humiliated, and contemplating suicide. This is particularly true when they are arrested at school for school-related offenses like talking back to their teacher, lewd behavior, disrupting a public school for a cat fight on a school bus, or smoking cigarettes in the girls' restroom. Many develop low esteem that is played out in hyper-sexuality, drug and alcohol abuse, and counterproductive behavior even after the charges are dismissed.

Like police, prosecutors must uphold the law. However, they can also be instrumental in decriminalization, diverting criminalization, determining the need for services of youth offenders, and delivering services to youthful offenders, especially girls who are victims of the sexual abuse and prostitution to prison pipeline. Prosecutors can protect girls and prevent future harm to girls based on the services that county and state governments can provide. For example, victims of human trafficking and domestic child sexual exploitation need safe houses not jailhouses. Victims of homelessness who engage in youthful offenses like stealing food or breaking and entering a vehicle to sleep at night require safe housing not a prison. Runaways and throwaways who are victims of physical, sexual, emotional and mental abuse require mental health services and shelter, not a prison environment that further victimizes them and uses penal and punitive measures for disciplinary reaction. According to the

Department of Justice Bureau of Statistic[3], girls are forcible sexually assaulted by jailers and juvenile detention staffers.

There are more than enough resources available for services. From federal commission reports to state and not-for profit studies, it cost more to arrest, charge, convict, and incarcerate than it does to educate, motivate, and stimulate the minds of our children, especial our girls. Systematic and institutionalized racism, sexism, and classism still exists and is prevalent. However, children have Constitution rights. Advocates must continue to be diligent and challenge abuses and violations of the rights of children.

#FemaleNOTFeemale: Prison (Rehabilitate)

Most readers of this book would agree that they regard their liberty as the foremost human right. However, this right may not become apparent until it is subject to deprivation. Every year thousands of women and girls are arrested, convicted, and incarcerated for alleged crimes in America. The disparities facing females of color is alarming. Women and girls of color represent less than 25% of the United States total population, but represent almost 50% of the US prison population. Millions of children in the United States have a parent who is either incarcerated or subject to penal supervision with almost 66% of incarcerated women having children[4].

Worth quoting, according to Families Against Mandatory Minimums (FAMM)[5]:
- ✓ 93 out of every 100,000 white women are incarcerated.
- ✓ The incarceration rate is four times higher for black women (380 of 100,000) and 1.6 times higher for Hispanic women (147 of 100,000).
- ✓ Whites only comprise 45.5% of female prisoners, even though whites are 79.8% of the United States population.
- ✓ By contrast, black women represent 32.6% of female prisoners, but only 12.8% of the general population.
- ✓ Black children are nearly 7.5 times more likely than white children to have a parent in prison.

Females represent the fastest growing members of the prison population[6]. Often, females are so busy advocating for the rights of men, that they get lost

---

[3] Beck. Alan. Sexual Victimization by Juvenile Facilities.
http://www.bjs.gov/content/pub/pdf/svjfry12.pdf (2013)
[4] Jefferson. Sherri. Prison Nation. www.wordpress.com/attorneysherrijefferson (2015)
[5] FAMM. Women in Prison in a Nutshell.
http://famm.org/Repository/Files/FS%20Women%20in%20Prisons%20in%20a%20Nutshell%206.25.10.pdf (March 26, 2016)
[6] Ajinkya, Julie. Rethinking How to Address the Growing Female Prison Population,
https://www.americanprogress.org/issues/women/news/2013/03/08/55787/rethinking-how-to-address-the-growing-female-prison-population/ (March 8, 2013); ACLU. Facts about the Over-Incarceration of Women in the United States. https://www.aclu.org/facts-about-over-

in their own conversations. Gender bias causes girls to be victims of ineffective assistance of counsel, bias enforcement of laws, sexism, racism, and indigent status. From prosecuting prostitutes to putting away runaways, America's continuing neglect of girls is alarming. America is a prison nation. From strip searches to sexual assaults, incarcerated girls are victims of mental, emotional, psychological, and physical abuse and neglect before, during and after incarceration and detention. In some jurisdictions, the rate of sexual victimization against youth in juvenile facilities is at least 35 percent higher than the average rate of correctional facilities across America.[7]

Respectfully, most female inmates are nonviolent offenders, some are victims of drug or alcohol abuse, and victims of sexual or physical abuse. Many of the female inmates have not attained high school diplomas or formal education. What has America to gain by incarcerating the most vulnerable segment of society?[8]

The privatization of the prison industrial complex has created a growing trend in the incarceration of women and girls. GEO and Corrections Corporation of America represent two of the largest for-profit prisons in the America. These private companies operate billion dollar enterprises, which require no governmental oversight concerning programs and services for treatment or rehabilitation. Therefore, women and girls who enter their systems are less likely to receive services which promote re-entry into society.

In our criminal justice system, females are more likely to be represented by public defenders. Most public defenders are not trained to address the issues that plague female inmates or have the resources to advocate for and negotiate pleas that address the underlying issues leading to arrest, conviction and incarceration. Unfortunately, women and girls are less likely to benefit from counsel after being arrested or accused of a crime. Evidence-based practices are almost never heard by judges because of time constraints placed upon lawyers during case presentment. Juvenile courts seldom entertain motion practice and some prosecutors charge children with the same vigor as they do adults. In some cases, it is all about attaining a conviction.

America's obsession with incarcerating its most vulnerable members of society should be of great concern to everyone because numerous studies prove that incarceration does not prevent crime or advance public safety. It is inexcusable to suffer the most disenfranchised segment of society to the harsh conditions of prison life. Moving forward our society should demand dismantling the "*from*

incarceration-women-united-states (March 26, 2016); FAMM. Women in Prison in a Nutshell. http://famm.org/Repository/Files/FS%20Women%20in%20Prisons%20in%20a%20Nutshell% 206.25.10.pdf (March 26, 2016)

[7] Id.

[8] Jefferson, Sherri. Id

my house to the courthouse to the jailhouse to be warehoused" mentality of the criminal justice system by promoting community and faith based initiatives. Girls require treatment and rehabilitation services to address their plights. We must work to end the growing trend of incarcerating women and girls in America. We must stop treating girls who are victims of sex crimes and prostitution as criminals as well as girls who are victims of abuse and neglect.[9]

The alternatives to the mass incarceration of girls is community and faith-based initiatives, which promotes treatment and counseling for drugs, mental health and alcohol, which provides life skills, education and employment services. Community based programs can allow girls to attend school during the regular school hours and report to treatment centers afterschool and on the weekends, like AA and NA programs. This method will not disrupt their home life. Removal of children from their homes for 30 – 90 days is traumatic. Conversely, local school districts can assign schools within their district to provide programs for girls as part of court-ordered treatment and rehabilitative programs. These courses can be added into their regular curriculum and required for their program completion. These courses can be available online or through traditional teaching methods. The classes to be taught can include drug and alcohol awareness, sex education, anger management and behavioral management. Restorative justice programs will aid in assisting victims of crimes to understand the mindset of the perpetrators and be willing to aid in rehabilitation where appropriate. Diversion and treatment programs work and we must address the issues that plague our most vulnerable members of society who are nonviolent offenders and can benefit from treatment.

#FemaleNOTFeemale: The Courthouse (Reassess)

The role of judges in deprivation and delinquency proceedings is to rule, reassess, and rebuild relationships with the child, school and community to ensure rehabilitation. Their role is critical to the pipelines and the scales of injustice because it is inside of the courthouse that decisions are made concerning resolution and deposition of deprivation and delinquency cases. Girls who require treatment and rehabilitation from physicians, psychologist and pharmaceutical personnel rely upon judges to make unbiased judicial decisions. When some judges engage in racism, sexism, classism, abuse of judicial misconduct and discretion, and use the bench to engage in judicial activism, they are a disservice and disgrace to the judiciary. Unfortunately, too many judges fit this category and it is a conversation that many people do not wish to engage.

---

[9] Jefferson, Sherri. Id

Well, we have to talk about it if we truly want to change the plight of our girls. Judges who are appointed or elected should be educated in programs and services available for girls. Judges should be screened by the 10 Ps prior to and subject to acceptance of appointments or to be elected as juvenile court and family judges. They should possess at least 7 years of experience in the field as practicing attorneys in juvenile justice and family law cases that emphasizes delinquency and deprivation. Ideally, judges should be elected to serve not appointed.

Nevertheless, once appointed or elected to serve judges should be required to impanel a board or panel consisting of the *10 Ps*. This panel should render a decision about the treatment and services of the child that must be considered by the judge before the he or she renders a decision to the detriment of the child. The panel should be present to hear cases and serve as the "jury" in juvenile court proceedings. The panel will serve to aid the court in offering recommendations for treatment and rehabilitation. For decades, we claimed that we were protecting children and maintaining confidentiality. We asserted that we would not authorize other people to attend court sessions. However, with zero tolerance, school arrest and media interaction, confidentiality and the interest of protecting youth do not exist. Today, children are arrested at school and subject to peer humiliation. Therefore, panels should be able to observe, serve, and make recommendations. These services are akin to the federal sentencing commission or the role of jurors in adult proceedings who hear evidence and deliberate. Where one person who works cooperatively with the prosecutors and police is the sole and final arbiter of decisions to the detriment of an accused, it will always create discriminatory and arbitrary enforcement of the law.

Too often, judges come to the bench with their own personal biases and their decision to detain a girl may be predicated upon those biases. Sure, there exist plenty of "evidence based" practices that are never considered by juvenile court judges or prosecutors. Most juvenile girls rely upon public defenders and the fast paced system we call justice that creates a revolving door that reads "return." Despite all of the research, our juvenile justice system does not prepare children, especially our girls for "re-entry" into society.

#FemaleNOTFeemale: The White House

Ideally, the White House is not one of the Houses that Raise Our Girls. However, it is the home to the President of the United States and our Commander-in-Chief. To that end, we look to the residents of the White House to aid in the dismantling of the schoolhouse to prison pipelines, the jailhouse to be warehoused realities that are experienced by youthful female offenders and to prepare and present an Executive Order to address these issues. The

White House is empowered to effectuate immediate action regarding human trafficking and domestic policies. Our girls need our government to protect their interest.

PROJECT *17Ps*

UNDERSTANDING HUMAN & SEX TRAFFICKING & ENDING DEMAND

PIMP, PANDERER, PROSTITUTE, PURCHASER, PROFITEER, PARENT, PASTOR, PRINCIPAL, POLICE, PROSECUTOR, PRISON, PHYSICIAN, PSYCHOLOGIST, PSYCHIATRIST, PHARMACEUTICAL, PRESS, AND POLITICIANS.

EPILOGUE

#FemaleNOTFeemale

The Leading Pipeline of Imprisonment of Girls in America

#FemaleNOTFeemale: Sexual Abuse and Prostitution (Human Trafficking and Child Sexual Exploitation)

Every day in America, thousands of women and children are sold for sex. Although we say "no such thing", law enforcement arrests the children as "juvenile prostitutes" and for prostitution related offenses asserting they are not victims but are willing participants. In major cities, girls are victims of sex trafficking. Human trafficking and the sexual exploitation of girls affects all races. However, in most major cities girls of color represent the majority of victims of sexual exploitation. This is not a new phenomenon. Since the new millennium, commercial sexual exploitation of girls has grown to become part of a billion-dollar industry. These children are bought, traded, sold and exchanged for sexual acts that include forced anal and oral sodomy. Many of these children are victims of gang rapes and are branded like slaves and animals prepared for slaughter.

Social Media has its advantages when used properly with parental guidance and oversight. However, too many of our youth have access to adult social media sites, chat rooms, and videos that are not monitored or governed by parents or the law enforcement community making them targets for predators.

Social media alone is not responsible for sex trafficking, however, its influence amongst society and the people who prey upon children calls upon them to be accountable and responsible for what happens to our children. In this techno-info era of non-communicative interactions, girls use the internet under an honor system that the person or persons engaging are of the same age. Yes. There are some who are well abreast that they may have gained access to an adult only site. However, most make clear that they called a chat line or entered a website for entertainment. Many assumed that they were conversing with someone of the same age and mind.

The tools used by social media users authorize the posting of pictures exposing nudity and using direct messaging aka "DMs" to interact with others via "bookings". Many social medias do not have safeguards to protect users from unsolicited attention. Many social media platforms do not require photos and verification of its users.

Unfortunately, social media is not the only tool that has failed to provide safeguards for youth. Television and music send the wrong message. The message sent to girls through videos and song is to strip off your clothes, engage in exotic dancing, and is lyrically hyper-sexual. Girls respond to these lyrics and engage in such acts.

Magazines, radio, and television also engages in negative stereotypes of defining beauty that makes some girls feel constrained to conform through plastic surgery, dressing provocatively, and engaging in hyper-sexual behavior. Alternatively, some girls feel neglected by their own communities whose focus is male-oriented. If you read a magazine, watch television, or listen to the radio and all you hear is how to support boys and men, then eventually you question your own self-worth.

For as long as most can remember, we have heard that mothers raise their daughters and love their sons. This paradigm has resulted in girls being vulnerable and developing unhealthy relationships.

Children for Sale?

Girls are being exploited by use of every medium of social media. The sexual norms of this generation and the exploitation through social media is beyond comprehension. From websites like ghetto gaggers to black crime, from back pages to after school app, from Instagram to Facebook, and Whisper to Vine girls are being convinced into selling their bodies and are victims of sexual exploitation. Many parents have no idea what their children are doing on social media platforms like Twitter, YouTube, Afterschool App, Kik, or Tinder, to name a few. From posting pictures of nudity to engaging in pornography our girls are witnessing and experiencing a transitional stage of life that no one can imagine.

Sexing and texting laws are methods used to curb the use of social media platforms for exploitation. However, the laws and the collateral consequences associated with arresting teenagers for posting or sending nude pictures causes more harm than good. The end result is embarrassment, shame, humiliation and a criminal record. A criminal record prohibits or grossly interferes with a girls' ability to attain her H.E.M.S[10]. Therefore, she is more inclined to enter

---

[10] Housing, Healthcare, Education, Employment, Maintenance and Support

into or remain in a life of prostitution. Too many judges are involved in judicial activism where they attempt to create their own laws from the bench. While legislators are engaged in moral legislation and activism. They create and enact laws to control lifestyles and life choices. In many regards, these laws have unintended consequences and create harm to girls.

Girls under the age of 18 have been recruited, transported and abused for purposes associated with sexual exploitation. America has remained silent while the lives of children are destroyed. Part of the mentality that thwarted prevention of exploitation and the intervention and delivery of services to these victims stem from racist, sexist and misogynist views of girls.

The pimps and traffickers lure young girls by being father figures offering moral support and gifts. In some regards, they will use male classmates to invite girls to their home to lure them into prostitution. Alternatively, teenage boys will pretend to be interested in the girls with hopes of luring her into a life of prostitution. They target young girls from foster care services and group homes as well as girls who are runaways and throwaways. Through the use of mental, emotional and psychological abuse they gain control of these children. Some of the girls are lured into a life of prostitution through threats of violence to family, loved ones, and physical attacks upon their person.

Many girls are exploited by African-American and Latino pimps. Some of the girls are lured into sexual exploitation through internet chat rooms, social media networks, and call-in telephone chat lines commercials available on music and reality shows on cable networks. Some of the victims of child sexual exploitation are as young as 10 years of age. One of the biggest myths associated with child exploitation is that the children are generally put on the streets to solicit sex. However, some attend school every day and meet their "Johns" after school in a private residence; some of the girls are picked up by their pimps on school campuses.

Other girls are exploited through "sex parties" that are hosted in private residences in suburban communities where white and foreign men pay a door rate of $50.00 to $100.00 to commit sexual acts upon as many boys and girls that are in attendance. These parties start as early as 9 am and end before normal school hours and the business day. We also recognize that children are lured into a life of sexual exploitation through false hopes of being the next video vixen to make appearances in music videos or becoming the next actress or supermodel.

The Cost of Silence

With this information, we must ask why are these girls arrested as juvenile prostitutes? The arrest, detention, and conviction of these children for prostitution have existed for more than two decades. The arrest has damaged thousands of innocent girls. While forced prostitution is a painful experience for all girls, girls of color are more likely to be arrested as juvenile prostitutes. One questions the role of race and the stereotypes associated with girls of color that falsely presume that they are hyper-sexualized beings. According to the most recent FBI report, 59.5%[11] of the girls arrested in the US are African-American girls. The emotional, mental, and psychological impact associated with arrest is profound. The impact of drugs, alcoholism, pregnancy, and sexual transmitted diseases represent the cost of silence. So what is being done to cause a traffic jam to stop human trafficking in America?

The 10 Ps[12] must address this issue with the Johns, pimps, and traffickers responsible for the exploitation[13] of women and children. The men and women responsible for pimping these girls must be held accountable and responsible for their actions. The pornography industry is controlled by white men. There exists an immediate response to the cries of young victims whose pimps and traffickers are men of color.

The Cost of Politics

Agencies across America have been recipients of grant funding to address the victimization of girls.

Over the course of a decade, the role of corporate financial supporters on issues like human trafficking and juvenile justice and reform, the role of the Black "powers that be," and the role of the political and nonprofit leaders who work effortlessly to thwart meaningful advocacy has made it impossible for some girls to receive services.

Grant funding is a multibillion dollar industry. Groups across this country receive millions of dollars to *conduct studies* and then write about the plights of girls in America. Respectfully, their research offers no change in the daily lives of girls. From funding organizations to those who profess dismantling the school to prison pipeline to addressing the detention of victims of child sexual exploitation and human trafficking, there exists no change in statistics that offer meaningful outcomes for girls.

We need to amend the Trafficking Victim Protection Act 2000 and the Justice for Victims of Trafficking Act 2015 to add three simple provisions that would end the arrest of children for prostitution, end unequal protection for boys and

---

[11] FBI 2012 report
[12] *Parents, Pastors, Principals, Police, Prosecutors and Prison and the Mental Health track: Physicians, Psychologist/Psychiatrist and Pharmaceutical. The Advocacy track: Politicians.*
[13] Boys and children who identify as members of the LGBT

LGBT and create a Fair Criminal Record Reporting Act to delete past arrest and conviction records to prevent collateral consequences associated with arrest.

Why should girls have to prove that they were not willing, knowing or intelligent participants of anal and oral sodomy, gang rape or that they never reaped a dime for engaging in commercial sexual acts? Instead of researching facts already known about these abuses, create laws that will effectuate actual change. Slavery, child labor, and prostitution are well verse topics in America. Criminal records should be deleted against children under 18 years of age charged or convicted of prostitution (or associated charges). To vacate their arrest means that they have to report it in response to educational, employment and housing inquiries.

Vacating an arrest or expungement of an arrest does not mean that the record is deleted. Like credit reporting services, Trans Union, Experian, and Equifax are vested with the authority to maintain credit histories. After seven (7) years credit histories are subject to deletion, bankruptcy is deleted after ten years. In America, a person can file bankruptcy and discharge millions of dollars in debt and after two years purchase a home or car. The same person could have a criminal record involving the possession of marijuana - a joint – or a theft of $50.00 from a retail store and their record will follow them for life. A Fair Criminal Records Reporting Act would authorize the deletion of records after several years, Two years for misdemeanors and after seven years for non-violent felony. America has the ability to delete their criminal records related to prostitution.

How Much Longer?

Since the 2000 enactment of the Trafficking Victims Protection Act, only 31 out of 50 states have enacted laws that govern the issue of trafficking, only 18 out of 50 states actually have *Safe Harbor* laws. Legislation should mandate that all states have a Safe Harbor law that protects victims of sexual exploitation, decriminalizes their victimization and offers and delivers programs and services. So we do not need any more research about the oldest plights and "professions" in America: slavery, child labor, and prostitution. We do not need white paper; we need results. We need programs. Jail is no place for victims of sexual exploitation.

The privatization of the prison industrial complex infringes upon and compromises the integrity of treatment and rehabilitation of victims of child sexual exploitation. America would rather pay for beds in jailhouses than finance beds for safe houses. Surely, we all know the collateral consequences of arresting victims of child sexual exploitation. We know that arrest is a traumatic experience and the inability to secure employment, educational opportunities as well as housing is compromised.

"You may choose to look the other way,

but you can never say again that you did not know."

-Williams Wilberforce

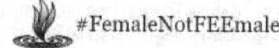 #FemaleNotFEEmale

Acknowledgements

Special thanks to the children and families whose experiences have taught me to pay-it forward! I will continue to be encouraged and I will advocate for you!

Special thanks to my family, friends, advocates and colleagues.

Author Sherri Jefferson

Sherri Jefferson is an author, independent book publisher, attorney, advocate, and lecturer. She is also the founder of the Family Law Center, African American Juvenile Justice Project, Jefferson Publishing, and the Law Mobile. Through #FemaleNOTFeemale, she advocates against child sexual exploitation and sex slavery, and the collateral consequences associated with criminalizing the acts of the victims of human trafficking and prostitution.

www.SherriJefferson.com

BEYOND THE BOOK: Reader's Circle

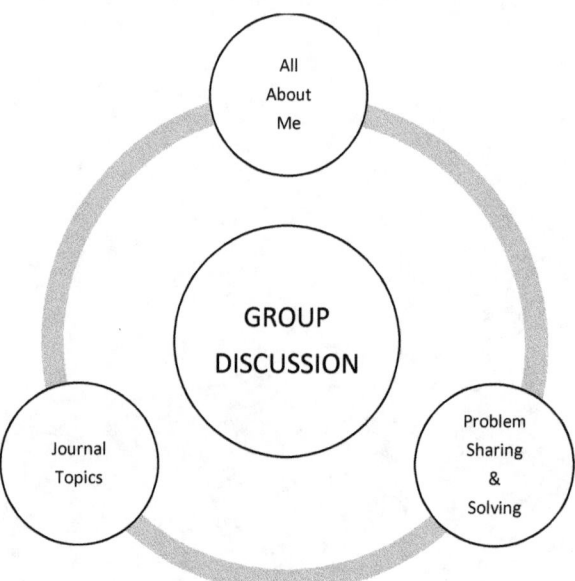

ADVOCACY

Politicians

CRIMINAL JUSTICE

Police, Prosecutor, Prison

MENTAL HEALTH

Physicians, *Psychiatrist, Pharmaceutical

*Psychologist

COMMUNITY

Parents, Pastors, Principals

PROJECT 10 Ps

Pimping, Pandering, and Prostitution

1 (888) 373-7888

National Human Trafficking Resource Center

SMS: 233733 (Text "HELP" or "INFO")
Hours: 24 hours, 7 days a week
Languages: English, Spanish and 200 more languages
Website: **traffickingresourcecenter.org**

THE 10 PS TO PIMPING, PANDERING & PROSTITUTION

Community: Parents, Pastors and Principals

1. What causes a child to grow up to be a pimp, prostitute or john?
2. What can parents do to prevent their children from becoming pimps, prostitutes, or Johns?
3. What is the role of pastors (church) in addressing pimping, prostitution and being a John and ending child sex slavery?
4. Why is the "Black Church" silent on the issue of child sex slavery in America?
5. What is the role of the principals (school) in educating students about pimping, prostitution and being a John?

Criminal Justice: Police Prosecutors and Prisons

1. Should police be authorized to arrest children as prostitutes?
2. Should victims of sex slavery be arrested or referred to social services/CPS?
3. Are police and prosecutors bias in handling juvenile prostitution and why?
4. Why are "Johns" who solicit sex from children not prosecuted as rapist and felons?
5. What should be the role of the police, prosecutor and prison system in dealing with sex slavery?

Mental Health: Physicians, Psychologist (Psychiatrist) and Pharmaceutical

1. Victims of sex slavery suffer from STDs, AIDS, abortions & physical torment.

Q.   What is the role of **physicians** in addressing public health issues associated with sex slavery?

2. Victims of sex slavery suffer from depression, anxiety, suicide, and addiction.

Q.   What is the role of the **mental health** community in addressing these issues?

3. Victims of sex slavery overdose on drugs, are addicted to drugs and are forced to use illicit drugs.

Q.   What is the role of the **pharmaceutical** industry in addressing drug abuse among victims of sex trafficking?

Advocate: Politicians

1. What is the role of politicians in ending sex slavery?
2. Why have politicians refused to enact **tough** laws to punish "Johns?"
3. Why did it take so many years for politicians to recognize victims of sex slavery in most jurisdictions?

UNDERSTANDING CHILD SEXUAL EXPLOITATION
& JUVENILE PROSTITUTION

Some Pipelines to Victimization of Sexual Abuse & Prostitution

1. Poverty
2. Dysfunctional home life
3. Educational failure
4. Neglect and abuse
5. Maltreatment and Mistreatment
6. Sexual/Physical Abuse
7. Emotional/Psychological problems
8. Housing instability and Homelessness
9. Runaways/Throwaways

Affiliations

1. Gangs.
2. Churches and Religious Organizations
3. School clubs

Tattoos on Body Parts: Crowns, Dollar Signs, Gangs Colors and Signs, etc.

1. Behind the ear
2. On the thighs and lower buttocks
3. On the arm and across the chest including bar codes and eagles, etc.
4. Marks on the face
5. Marks on the ankle
6. Letters across the fingers or a cross on the neck

GROUP DISCUSSION & PROBLEM SHARING
AND PROBLEM SOLVING

1. Help your female get to the next level
2. Help your female to discover who they are without being judgmental
3. Encourage your female to engage in self-examination
4. When is judging **not** being judgmental?
5. Keeping it 'real' or '100' means?
6. Your female really has an addiction. Now what?
7. Discussing HIV/AIDS with a female victim of human trafficking.
8. Discussing and understanding victims of the school to prison pipeline.
9. Character flaws v. Flawed Character
10. Developing lasting female friendships.
11. Your female friend is not perfect and neither are you.
12. Knowing the difference between forgiving and forgetting.
13. Second chance or Fair Chance.
14. A Change or A Chance.

ALL ABOUT ME

1. Discover who I am.
2. Rediscover who I am and what I am destined to be in this world.
3. Redefine, reorganize and reprioritize what is truly important to me.
4. Why am I "this" or "that" way?
5. Am I capable of changing and if so why or why not?
6. What must I do to better my own life?
7. Who owes me and why?
8. Life. What does it really mean?
9. My future. I see myself in 3-5 years (5-7, 7-10, 10-15 years) doing . . .
10. Before I can become a friend to someone else, I must befriend myself. So how do I accomplish this goal?
11. A friend is . . .?
12. Why do I need friends in my life?
13. What are the benefits of this "friendship" and what do I bring to or take away from the friendship?
14. What makes me unique?
15. My past does not determine my future . . .
16. I must learn to forgive myself because . . .

ACTIVITIES

1. Project Stay in Touch (adopt a juvenile detention center, girls' detention - send cards, letters of encouragement, etc.)
2. Start a support group at your school, church, or community for former incarcerated children or children of incarcerated parents.
3. Mentor
4. Volunteer at established programs
5. Support community and faith-based prison ministry
6. Start a Project 6Ps or 10 Ps in your home, school, church, or community
7. Advocate against the school-to-prison pipeline or human trafficking
8. Is there a difference between sex trafficking and prostitution?
9. Are some prostitutes willing participants who knowingly sell for profit?
10. Are exotic dancers, video vixens, or porn stars victims of human trafficking?
11. Create petitions to bring awareness
12. Host family night or host game night
13. Host a family for food, fun, and fellowship day/night
14. Create an awareness program for foster care and services
15. Become a foster parent or adopt a child
16. Advocate for video conferencing in prison and the reduction of the cost associated with calling and staying in touch with loved ones who are incarcerated
17. Advocate for reduction of cost of commissary items or for the ability to purchase items through vendors of choice for less money
18. Advocate against telecommunication companies who charge enormous fees for per minute telephone calls and for every person incarcerated to be able to have an email account (like CORRS system)
19. Advocate for schools to remain open during summer breaks and holidays as a safe haven for families in need of child care services
20. Advocate for summer employment programs
21. Advocate for community based lunch and dinner programs during the school year and breakfast, lunch and dinner programs during the summer
22. Advocate for funding for arts and music programs
23. Advocate for community and recreational centers to remain open
24. Advocate for a Fair Criminal Records Reporting Act that would delete non-violent criminal records after a period – as credit reports delete histories.
25. Advocate for re-entry and second chance program 'Project Fresh Start'.

ESSAY TOPICS

1. Social Reform vs. Social Programs
2. Criminal Justice Reform
3. How can the 6Ps or 10 Ps (parents, pastors, principal, police, prosecutors and police) help to prevent human trafficking in America?
4. Explain the privatization of the prison industrial complex. Does for-profit prison prevent criminal justice reform?
5. Corruption, Racism, Abuse and Politics (CRAP)
6. Discuss the women's suffrage movement and the struggles of African American women in America or Latina women.
7. Is the criminal justice system color blind or blinded by color?
8. If you were the President, what would your plan against Human Trafficking and the War on Girls be for America?
9. Compare and contrast girls from the 1960s to youth of today.
10. Choose a decade and write about the progress of females in America.
11. Advocate for a Fair Criminal Records Reporting Act that would delete non-violent criminal records after a period – as credit reports delete histories. Re-entry and second chance program 'Project Fresh Start'.
12. Identify the struggles of Black females in America in the 1960s and today.
13. Discuss Martha Griffith and the Equal Rights Amendment.
14. Discuss Shirley Chisolm and Hillary R. Clinton's Presidential campaigns.
15. Choose two First Ladies of the United States and compare and contrast their advocacy for the rights of Americans during their husband's presidential terms.